Teamwork

READING
Test Practice

GRADE

4

Carson-Dellosa Publishing Company, Inc.
Greensboro, North Carolina

Introduction

Teamwork Reading Test Practice is designed to provide students with test-taking practice by introducing them to the format and content of the standardized tests they will encounter. This book does not replace effective teaching strategies, but rather it supplements the classroom teacher's existing curriculum and provides testing practice that will enable students to demonstrate what they have learned. Each practice test addresses the main reading objectives and student expectations for fourth grade. The matrix on pages 4–5 conveniently references the standard and skills addressed in each question. Cross-curricular instructional strategies and engaging skill-based activities that have been correlated with standards are provided in *Teamwork Test Prep—Grade 4* (CD-2237). A specific section on test-taking strategies is also included in the teacher resource book.

This book contains a variety of reading selections and corresponding practice tests. Designed to provide a wide range of backgrounds, perspectives, and topics, the reading selections reflect the kinds of passages fourth-grade students are expected to read and understand.

Following the reading passages are multiple-choice questions that address the general reading standards that are representative of most states' standards. The tests are similar in format to standardized tests fourth-grade students will encounter. Some tests include a question that requires a short written response. A grid and bubble answer sheet is included on page 47 to familiarize students with tracking. *Note: Remind students to cross out any row of answer bubbles that will not be used depending on the test they are taking.*

Credits

Project Director: Melissa S.Hughes, M.A.Ed., M.S.Ed.
Editors: Karen Seberg, Debra Olson Pressnall, and Kathryn Wheeler
Graphic Layout: Mark Conrad
Inside Illustrations: Tim Foley
Cover Design: Annette Hollister-Papp and Peggy Jackson

Teacher Reviewers:

Deborah Plumb, Grade 4 Teacher
Irving Independent School District, Texas

Jeanette Spinale, Educational Consultant
University of Massachusetts Dartmouth

Printed in the USA • All rights reserved.

ISBN: 1-59441-145-X

Table of Contents

Matrix of Objectives and Skills

Test Question Addressing Each Skill

	Skills	Mike and Moe	Neighbors	Sharks	Emilio's Tadpoles	The Midnight Ride	Saguaro Cactus	A Field Trip to the Recycling Center	Stained Light	A Class Trip to the Zoo	Another Use for Seeds	Amelia Earhart
Objective 1 — The student will demonstrate a basic understanding of vocabulary and concept development in diverse texts.	Acquire vocabulary through word study, context clues, and reference aids	5, 6		7, 11	2	2, 4	3, 5	11	1	2	2	1
	Identify word origins, roots, prefixes, and suffixes		12					2	9	13		
	Recognize synonyms and antonyms		2, 7	2, 3	1, 10		1	15	2			
	Recognize homophones and homographs								13	15	8	6
	Differentiate between multiple meanings of words	12		12		12		1, 3	15	7		12
	Determine main ideas and supporting details	3	4	4, 13	7, 14	1, 7	2, 9	13	7, 10	5, 8	3, 10	7, 10
	Paraphrase and summarize texts						13		8	1	1	
Objective 2 — The student will apply knowledge of literary elements to understand diverse texts.	Recognize genres and distinguishing features of various types of texts	8		1			4		3			11
	Recognize and analyze elements of characterization		1, 5		12			8	14	12		2, 5
	Recognize and analyze story setting				5	9		7	4	9		
	Recognize and analyze story plot		3								11	

Skill											
Recognize and analyze story resolution				8							
Identify the speaker or narrator	2		10								
Objective 3 — The student will use a variety of strategies to analyze structural features of diverse texts.											
Use text features to locate information	4										
Distinguish between fact and opinion			9	4			4	6, 11	11	6	4
Identify cause and effect relationships			9	3	3	8	9	12	14	7	
Identify chronology of events		11		13	8		14				
Identify similarities and differences		10, 13	8								
Represent text information in various forms						11	10				
Identify purposes of texts	1		5			6	12		3		3
Use prior knowledge to make connections with new material					11					12	
Recognize and understand the use of figurative language				9		12					
Objective 4 — The student will apply critical thinking skills to analyze diverse texts.											
Draw inferences and support with text evidence	7	6	6	6, 11, 15	5	7	5	5	6	4, 5, 9	8, 9
Connect, compare, and contrast ideas, themes, and issues					6, 10	10					
Recognize methods of organizing information		6							4		
Make predictions			11	16			6		10		

5

Practice Vocabulary Test 1

Choose the word that has the SAME meaning as the underlined word.

1   There was no <u>movement</u> in the house.

    Ⓐ advance   Ⓒ attach

    Ⓑ motion   Ⓓ avoid

2   Carlos didn't <u>hesitate</u> to ride the roller coaster.

    Ⓕ quiver   Ⓗ cancel

    Ⓖ vibrate   Ⓙ pause

3   I was <u>disappointed</u> that we couldn't go.

    Ⓐ upset   Ⓒ relieved

    Ⓑ proud   Ⓓ angry

Choose the word that has the OPPOSITE meaning of the underlined word.

4   Chloe <u>admired</u> Miss Jensen because she was such a good teacher.

    Ⓕ believed   Ⓗ disapproved of

    Ⓖ promised   Ⓙ respected

5   We arrived at the field <u>promptly</u> at 6:00.

    Ⓐ quick   Ⓒ sorry

    Ⓑ late   Ⓓ timely

6   It was <u>routine</u> to walk the dog every day.

    Ⓕ usual   Ⓗ daily

    Ⓖ unusual   Ⓙ skillful

7   The dog was <u>enormous</u>.

    Ⓐ pretty   Ⓒ tiny

    Ⓑ scary   Ⓓ active

Choose the correct definition for the underlined word as used in the sentence.

8   The president of the company was proud to <u>present</u> the new products at the meeting.

    Ⓕ a gift

    Ⓖ to show or display something

    Ⓗ to introduce someone formally

    Ⓙ taking place or existing now

9   Jasmine saw a tiny <u>crack</u> in the bottom of the vase.

    Ⓐ to solve a puzzle or a code

    Ⓑ a break or flaw in something

    Ⓒ to break into pieces

    Ⓓ a loud, sharp sound

10   We saw <u>odd</u> animal tracks in the woods.

    Ⓕ leftover   Ⓗ strange

    Ⓖ uneven   Ⓙ occasional

11   It was cool enough to wear a <u>light</u> jacket.

    Ⓐ pale in color

    Ⓑ lamp

    Ⓒ not very filling

    Ⓓ made of thin fabric

12   You should <u>file</u> the rough edges of the new birdhouse before you paint it.

    Ⓕ a metal tool

    Ⓖ a collection of related papers

    Ⓗ a line of people or things

    Ⓙ to smooth the surface of something

Practice Vocabulary Test 2

Choose the word that has the SAME meaning as the underlined word.

1 Strawberry was <u>definitely</u> Caroline's favorite flavor.

   Ⓐ lively   Ⓒ creatively

   Ⓑ absolutely   Ⓓ gratefully

2 It was <u>probable</u> that the park would be open.

   Ⓕ unlikely   Ⓗ honestly

   Ⓖ likely   Ⓙ playful

3 Melinda planted a <u>variety</u> of flowers.

   Ⓐ assortment   Ⓒ remarkable

   Ⓑ summary   Ⓓ likeness

4 Zoe <u>clutched</u> her backpack tightly.

   Ⓕ threw   Ⓗ grasped

   Ⓖ closed   Ⓙ punched

Choose the BEST word to complete each sentence.

5 Jermaine is a _____ member of our team.

   Ⓐ accurate   Ⓒ coach

   Ⓑ exercise   Ⓓ valuable

6 The streets were quiet and _____.

   Ⓕ stranded   Ⓗ deserted

   Ⓖ powerful   Ⓙ entrance

7 She asked the students not to _____ paper.

   Ⓐ type   Ⓒ waste

   Ⓑ complete   Ⓓ similar

Choose the BEST word to complete each sentence from the choices below.

Astronomy is one of Dayton's **(8)**_____ subjects. He likes to **(9)**_____ the movement of the stars. Dayton was happy when his parents gave him a **(10)**_____ for his birthday. On the first clear night, Tom was ready to make careful **(11)**_____ of the stars. He drew pictures of the Big Dipper in his **(12)**_____.

8   Ⓕ famous   Ⓗ favorite

        Ⓖ almost   Ⓙ similar

9   Ⓐ permit   Ⓒ study

        Ⓑ stencil   Ⓓ plan

10   Ⓕ telescope   Ⓗ microscope

        Ⓖ telegraph   Ⓙ telephone

11   Ⓐ stations   Ⓒ reservations

        Ⓑ situations   Ⓓ observations

12   Ⓕ textbook   Ⓗ atlas

        Ⓖ newspaper   Ⓙ journal

Practice Vocabulary Test 3

Choose the BEST word to complete each analogy.

1 Friend is to companion as story is to _____.

   Ⓐ library   Ⓒ book

   Ⓑ tale   Ⓓ castle

2 True is to false as freezing is to _____.

   Ⓕ snow   Ⓗ boiling

   Ⓖ water   Ⓙ weather

3 Fearful is to afraid as save is to _____.

   Ⓐ loss   Ⓒ cheap

   Ⓑ collect   Ⓓ afford

Choose the correct word to complete each sentence.

4 My mom put a juicy _____ in my lunch.

   Ⓕ pair   Ⓗ pare

   Ⓖ pear   Ⓙ par

5 Jean wanted to _____ a new skateboard.

   Ⓐ bye   Ⓒ buy

   Ⓑ by   Ⓓ byte

6 The candles had wonderful _____.

   Ⓕ sense   Ⓗ scents

   Ⓖ cents   Ⓙ scenes

7 They were hungry and _____.

   Ⓐ pore   Ⓒ pure

   Ⓑ poor   Ⓓ pour

Choose the BEST word to complete each sentence from the choices below.

Beavers are good swimmers. They are at home both on land and under the **(8)**_____. They spend their lives around streams. Beavers eat the soft inner bark of **(9)**_____ and trees that grow near the water. Maybe you have heard the **(10)**_____ "busy as a beaver." During the late summer and early **(11)**_____, the beavers are very busy indeed. They store supplies of branches and sticks under the water. When winter arrives they don't **(12)**_____ like some mammals. They swim out under the ice to get the food they have saved.

8   Ⓕ ground   Ⓗ air

       Ⓖ ocean   Ⓙ water

9   Ⓐ bushes   Ⓒ flowers

       Ⓑ mushrooms   Ⓓ leaves

10   Ⓕ fable   Ⓗ saying

       Ⓖ story   Ⓙ report

11   Ⓐ spring   Ⓒ year

       Ⓑ fall   Ⓓ winter

12   Ⓕ navigate   Ⓗ designate

       Ⓖ activate   Ⓙ hibernate

Directions: Read the story. Then answer questions 1 through 13.

(1) Mike was our first cat. We adopted him from the animal shelter when he was only eight weeks old. His fur was mostly white, but he had some orange stripes. From the beginning, Mike was a very independent kitten. He came to us when he wanted to be with people. When he wanted to be alone, he curled up in a laundry basket in the basement. Mike grew to be a pretty good-sized cat, and he ruled our house. Since he was our only pet, Mike received a lot of attention.

(2) That all changed the day we found Moe. Or maybe I should say the day Moe found us. It happened when Mike was about two years old. I was sitting on our patio reading when I thought I heard a cry. I looked under the chairs, on the other side of the wall around the patio, and even in the bushes, but I didn't see anything. The crying persisted. Finally, I looked up. There, about three feet above where I had been sitting, was a scrawny white kitten. He was hanging on for dear life to a skinny tree branch. I could tell the kitten was really scared, and I tried to reach the branch to help him down. But the branch was too high.

(3) I called for my brother Chris to bring a ladder. Together, we leaned the ladder against the tree. While I steadied the ladder, Chris carefully climbed up the first two rungs and reached for the kitten. Gently, he pulled him from the branch. Then he handed him down to me. He was the tiniest kitten I had ever seen. As I held him, the kitten stopped crying, but he was still trembling.

(4) We took the kitten to our veterinarian, who said the kitten was probably about four weeks old. She told us we would need to feed him a special formula with an eyedropper. Kittens eat a lot! We fed him that way for a few weeks until he was old enough to drink from a dish. As the kitten got bigger and began to fill out, he started to look a little like Mike, but without Mike's orange stripes. We named the kitten Moe.

(5) At first, Mike wasn't very nice to Moe. He wouldn't play with Moe, and he didn't like sharing his food either. Sometimes he would even hiss if Moe got too close. After a while, Mike seemed to decide he would just ignore Moe. But now I think Mike accepts him. After all, Moe is only half Mike's size and is scared of his own shadow. We have no idea how Moe came to be in that tree, but we are glad he was. We think maybe Mike is, too.

GO ON ➡

Practice Reading Test 4—Mike and Moe

1 This story was written mainly to—

Ⓐ tell about the author's two cats.

Ⓑ explain the best way to choose a pet.

Ⓒ explain how to get a kitten out of a tree.

Ⓓ describe how to care for a kitten.

2 Who is telling this story?

Ⓕ Chris

Ⓖ Chris's brother

Ⓗ Chris's sister

Ⓘ either G or H

3 Moe had to be fed with an eyedropper for ____ before he learned to drink from a dish.

Ⓐ a few hours

Ⓑ a few days

Ⓒ a few weeks

Ⓓ a few months

4 Which paragraph should you read to learn about the day the author found Moe?

Ⓕ paragraph 1

Ⓖ paragraph 2

Ⓗ paragraph 3

Ⓘ paragraph 4

5 Read this sentence from paragraph 1.

From the beginning, Mike was a very independent kitten.

What does the word **independent** mean?

Ⓐ wanted to be with people all of the time

Ⓑ was happy being alone sometimes

Ⓒ needed constant care

Ⓓ had a big appetite

6 When Moe was stuck in the tree, his crying **persisted**.

This means that his crying—

Ⓕ got louder.

Ⓖ stopped.

Ⓗ got softer.

Ⓘ continued.

7 Why was Moe was taken to a veterinarian?

Ⓐ because he was sick

Ⓑ because he wouldn't stop crying

Ⓒ because he was so young

Ⓓ because he couldn't walk

GO ON

Practice Reading Test 4—Mike and Moe

8 This story is an example of—

    Ⓕ historical fiction.

    Ⓖ a narrative.

    Ⓗ science fiction.

    Ⓙ a fable.

9 The author used phrase "scared of his own shadow" to describe Moe. This means that Moe is—

    Ⓐ afraid of the dark.

    Ⓑ afraid of shadows.

    Ⓒ very nervous.

    Ⓓ lonely.

10 One difference between Mike and Moe is—

    Ⓕ how they look.

    Ⓖ what they eat.

    Ⓗ when they sleep.

    Ⓙ where they live.

11 Which event happened first?

    Ⓐ Chris climbed a ladder to rescue the kitten.

    Ⓑ They took the kitten to the veterinarian.

    Ⓒ The kitten was stuck in the tree.

    Ⓓ They named the kitten Moe.

12 Read this sentence from paragraph 1.

Mike grew to be a pretty good-sized cat, and he ruled our house.

What does the word **ruled** mean?

    Ⓕ made a straight line

    Ⓖ controlled or had power over

    Ⓗ made a legal decision

    Ⓙ measured

13 SHORT ANSWER: Answer the following question on a separate sheet of paper. Use complete sentences.

How are Mike and Moe alike and different? Create a Venn diagram to show how they are similar and how they are different.

Directions: Read the story. Then answer questions 1 through 12.

Neighbors Need Neighbors

(1) Once, there was an old lady who lived on the edge of town. No one knew her name, but everyone called her Granny. Because she kept to herself, some people thought she was a little different. Granny didn't seem to have any friends or relatives. No one ever stopped by to visit her. She asked nothing of anyone and did nothing for anyone, with one exception. Granny took care of many dogs. The number of dogs changed daily. Some came only when they were hungry, then left until they returned to eat again. Others knew a good home when they saw it and decided to stay. Granny always made sure there was plenty of food and water for all of the dogs.

(2) James delivered newspapers in Granny's neighborhood. One day, he noticed that Granny's newspaper from the day before was still on the porch. The dogs in her yard were acting differently, too. They weren't resting in the shade. Most of them were running back and forth and barking. He looked around the yard and saw that their food dishes were empty. It wasn't like Granny not to feed her dogs. James realized that he had not seen Granny at all the day before. He wondered if she was all right.

(3) James got off his bike and walked up the steps onto the front porch. He peered in the front windows, but he didn't see anyone. Then he knocked on the front door but didn't hear any movement inside. Finally, he pulled on the door's handle. The door was unlocked. James opened it slightly and called, "Hello! Anyone here?"

(4) He listened for a minute—was that a whimpering sound? James ran back to his bike and rode as fast as he could to the closest neighbor's house, where he called 9-1-1. Then he raced back to Granny's house to wait for help.

GO ON →

Practice Reading Test 5—Neighbors Need Neighbors

(5) When the police arrived, they found that Granny had fallen and had not been able to move or call for help. The paramedics came just a few minutes later. They examined Granny and determined that she needed to go to the hospital. James asked when Granny would be coming home. One of the paramedics told him she would probably need to stay in the hospital for a few days.

(6) While Granny was in the hospital, James stopped by her house every day to care for the dogs. He made sure they had plenty of water and food. When Granny came home, some of the neighbors brought her meals. Others brought her flowers. Someone checked on her every night to see if she needed anything. Granny was grateful that James had taken care of her dogs. She was also sorry she hadn't gotten to know her new friends sooner, but now she was glad that they had found each other.

1 Which word describes Granny in the beginning of the story?

    Ⓐ worried

    Ⓑ friendly

    Ⓒ private

    Ⓓ mean

2 What does the word **peered** mean in paragraph 3?

    Ⓕ looked

    Ⓖ climbed

    Ⓗ listened

    Ⓙ jumped

3 Which event made James think that something might be wrong with Granny?

    Ⓐ The dogs were missing.

    Ⓑ Granny's newspaper had not been picked up.

    Ⓒ The paramedics were at Granny's house.

    Ⓓ Neighbors took food and flowers to Granny's house.

4 Paragraph 3 is mostly about—

    Ⓕ how James looked for Granny.

    Ⓖ why Granny kept to herself.

    Ⓗ what happened after James called 9-1-1.

    Ⓙ Granny's dogs.

GO ON

Practice Reading Test 5—Neighbors Need Neighbors

5 When James opened Granny's front door, he was—

 Ⓐ being nosy.

 Ⓑ concerned.

 Ⓒ trying to sneak up on Granny.

 Ⓓ irresponsible.

6 Why did James call 9-1-1?

 Ⓕ Someone had broken into Granny's house.

 Ⓖ He thought he heard someone whimpering.

 Ⓗ Granny's dogs had not been fed.

 Ⓙ Granny asked him to call for help.

7 Which word means the same as the word **determined** in paragraph 5?

 Ⓐ decided

 Ⓑ explained

 Ⓒ questioned

 Ⓓ drove

8 The author probably wrote this story to—

 Ⓕ inform readers about how to care for dogs.

 Ⓖ explain the responsibilities of paper carriers.

 Ⓗ show how important it is to have good neighbors.

 Ⓙ explain how to call 9-1-1.

9 Which sentence is an opinion?

 Ⓐ James delivers newspapers in his neighborhood.

 Ⓑ James thought something might be wrong with Granny and called 9-1-1.

 Ⓒ James cared for Granny's dogs while she was in the hospital.

 Ⓓ James is a wonderful friend.

10 At the end of the story, how does Granny feel about her neighbors?

 Ⓕ bothered by them

 Ⓖ angry with them

 Ⓗ sorry for them

 Ⓙ grateful to them

11 After Granny recovers, she will probably be—

 Ⓐ more private.

 Ⓑ angry with her neighbors.

 Ⓒ friendlier to her neighbors.

 Ⓓ afraid of her neighbors.

12 Which word from the story contains a suffix?

 Ⓕ newspaper

 Ⓖ movement

 Ⓗ police

 Ⓙ neighbor

STOP

Directions: Read the article. Then answer questions 1 through 13.

Sharks

(1) When you hear the word shark, do you think of a scary animal that attacks people ruthlessly? Over the years, the shark has gotten a bad reputation. In reality, there are fewer than 12 deaths from shark attacks in any one year. A person has a much greater chance of being struck by lightning than of being attacked by a shark. If people understood sharks better, they might not be so afraid of this fascinating ocean fish.

(2) Sharks have been around for millions of years. They even existed before the dinosaurs! Today there are over 350 different species of sharks. Some sharks are large and live in the open ocean. Other sharks are small and live near the ocean floor. Some sharks are fast swimmers and active hunters, while others are slow creatures that eat tiny fish.

(3) Sharks are fish but, unlike most fish, they do not have bony skeletons. They are mostly muscle with flexible skeletons of soft cartilage. Most fish have gill flaps that force water and oxygen through their gills. Sharks have open gill slits. This means most sharks must move constantly in the water in order to breathe. As they swim, the oxygen-rich water flows through their gills. If a shark gets trapped in a net, it can quickly drown.

(4) Some sharks, such as the tiger shark, hammerhead shark, and great white shark, are fierce hunters. Unless there is a lot of prey in an area, sharks usually hunt alone. A shark can sense sudden movement in the water and smell its prey with its excellent sense of smell. Sharks might hunt fish, turtles, seals, dolphins, and even other small sharks. When a human is attacked, most likely it's a case of mistaken identity. The shark may have thought the person was a sea lion. Sometimes a shark will attack to warn a human to stay out of its territory. Most people do survive shark attacks. The shark usually bites and then swims away.

(5) Many sharks are gentle, harmless fish. The whale shark may grow to be 40 feet (12 meters) long. Despite its size, this giant eats plankton, which is made up of tiny floating plants and animals. The smallest sharks are just a few inches long and eat shrimp and tiny fish.

(6) Some species of sharks are disappearing. Unfortunately, because sharks are feared, they have been greatly hunted. Sharks are also valued for their meat, skin, and oil. Each year, large numbers of sharks are caught accidentally in nets meant for other fish. Water pollution is also killing sharks, along with other forms of sea life. People today are learning more so they can save the sharks. These fish have been a part of ocean life for millions of years, and they deserve to be protected.

GO ON

Practice Reading Test 6—Sharks

1   This article is—

   Ⓐ informational.

   Ⓑ fictional.

   Ⓒ biographical.

   Ⓓ historical.

2   Which of the following words is an antonym for the word **constantly** in paragraph 3?

   Ⓕ regularly

   Ⓖ occasionally

   Ⓗ continually

   Ⓙ frequently

3   Which of the following words is a synonym for the word **gentle** in paragraph 5?

   Ⓐ restless

   Ⓑ troubled

   Ⓒ calm

   Ⓓ fierce

4   Which of the following books do you think would have the MOST information about sharks?

   Ⓕ *Ocean Life*

   Ⓖ *The World of Fish*

   Ⓗ *Sharks in the Seas*

   Ⓙ *Endangered Species of the Oceans*

5   The author probably wrote this article to—

   Ⓐ encourage people to become oceanographers.

   Ⓑ save a disappearing species.

   Ⓒ share some unique features of sharks.

   Ⓓ compare sharks with other fish.

6   Where does the author give information about false beliefs people have about sharks?

   Ⓕ the introduction

   Ⓖ the conclusion

   Ⓗ paragraph 2

   Ⓙ paragraph 5

7   In which of the following sentences is the word **attack** used as a noun?

   Ⓐ Many people think that sharks like to attack humans.

   Ⓑ It is uncommon for sharks to attack people.

   Ⓒ A person would probably not die from a shark attack.

   Ⓓ Sharks might attack when they sense danger.

Practice Reading Test 6—Sharks

8 How are sharks different from other fish?

  Ⓕ Sharks have gill flaps.

  Ⓖ Sharks are valued for their meat.

  Ⓗ Sharks do not have bony skeletons.

  Ⓙ Sharks eat other fish.

9 Which of the following is NOT a cause for the decline of the shark population?

  Ⓐ Many people hunt sharks because they are afraid of them.

  Ⓑ Sharks have been around for millions of years.

  Ⓒ Sharks drown in fishing nets because they must move to breathe.

  Ⓓ Sharks are valued for their meat, skin, and oil.

10 Which of the following statements is a fact?

  Ⓕ Sharks are the most interesting ocean animal to study.

  Ⓖ There are over 350 different species of sharks.

  Ⓗ People should try to save sharks.

  Ⓙ Water pollution is the worst form of pollution on earth.

11 Read this sentence from paragraph 1.

Over the years, the shark has gotten a bad reputation.

What does the word **reputation** mean?

  Ⓐ an opinion that people have about something

  Ⓑ a response to a question

  Ⓒ research about an ocean animal

  Ⓓ an explanation

12 Read this sentence from paragraph 3.

Most fish have gill flaps that force water and oxygen through their gills.

Which of the following is the correct definition for the word **flaps** in this sentence?

  Ⓕ to move something up and down

  Ⓖ to toss something

  Ⓗ a flat, thin cover

  Ⓙ the inside of a book's cover

13 SHORT ANSWER: Complete the following on a separate sheet of paper.

Identify the main ideas of this article. Make an outline using key words and phrases from the selection.

Directions: Read the story. Then answer questions 1 through 16.

Emilio's Tadpoles

(1) Emilio sat cross-legged by the window. He stared out at the foggy eucalyptus woods, wishing he was back in New Mexico with Carlos and Jose. Carlos and Jose were Emilio's two best friends back home. He thought about how much fun they had together. They loved to play air hockey and video games together. Sometimes they went hiking or rode their bikes to the park to play.

(2) He missed his old house and his old friends in New Mexico. His family had moved to Santa Barbara, California, just after Christmas. In two whole months, he hadn't made even one new friend. He felt selfish for being sad. Everyone else in his family was so happy to be in California, living by the ocean.

(3) His five-year-old sister, Socorro, seemed to like her new school. She had even found a kitten in the woods, and Mom and Dad had let her keep it. Dad had a great new job at the television station. He loved talking about all the celebrities he met. Mom liked California, too. She ran on the beach every morning and took classes at the community college in the afternoon.

(4) Emilio tried to make new friends, but he didn't know how. None of the boys in his class lived nearby. Besides, they all had been together since kindergarten. Emilio was an outsider. The boys were polite enough, even a little bit friendly, but after they said "hello" in the morning, they wandered off in their own groups. They never included him. Emilio couldn't blame them. He and his old friends had done the same thing lots of times.

(5) After a while, Emilio decided to stop feeling sorry for himself. Friends or no friends, it was a perfectly good Saturday afternoon. Emilio opened the sliding door and stepped out onto the deck. He felt better immediately. He took a deep breath and felt the warm sun on his face. The tall, shaggy-barked trees smelled like spices in the damp sea air.

GO ON ➡

Practice Reading Test 7—Emilio's Tadpoles

(6) He took the back steps two at a time. A carpet of fallen leaves shaped like feathers cushioned his steps as he jogged down the path to the nearby creek. But he was surprised when he got there. No water tumbled over the rocks. Small, stagnant ponds dotted the dry streambed.

(7) He looked more carefully into one of the little pools and noticed that it was teeming with tiny, dark swimmers. They were so close together they could hardly move. Tadpoles! A few had back legs, but Emilio could see they weren't ready to live on land. Unfortunately, the little bit of water left in the pools was evaporating fast. Suddenly, Emilio understood why everyone on the news was talking about the drought.

(8) Emilio couldn't make it rain, but he could help some of the tadpoles. He ran back to the house to get a plastic jar.

1 Read this sentence from paragraph 2.

He felt selfish for being sad.

What does the word **selfish** mean?

- Ⓐ lonely
- Ⓑ frightened
- Ⓒ self-centered
- Ⓓ excited

2 Read this sentence from paragraph 4.

Emilio was an outsider.

This means Emilio—

- Ⓕ felt like he wasn't part of the group.
- Ⓖ liked to spend time outdoors.
- Ⓗ wanted to be in a camping club.
- Ⓙ enjoyed studying nature.

3 Read the following sentence from paragraph 2 in the story.

In two whole months, he hadn't made even one new friend.

How did this fact affect Emilio?

- Ⓐ Emilio felt very lonely.
- Ⓑ Emilio felt like an outsider.
- Ⓒ Emilio had no one to play with.
- Ⓓ all of the above

4 Which sentence expresses an opinion?

Ⓕ Santa Barbara is in California.

Ⓖ Tadpoles grow into frogs.

Ⓗ It is always hard to make new friends.

Ⓘ A drought is caused by a lack of rain.

5 The story takes place—

Ⓐ at the creek near Emilio's house.

Ⓑ at Emilio's school.

Ⓒ inside Emilio's new house.

Ⓓ A and C

6 Which sentence shows that Emilio was feeling better?

Ⓕ Emilio sat cross-legged by the window.

Ⓖ Emilio was an outsider.

Ⓗ Emilio took the back steps two at a time.

Ⓘ Emilio understood why everyone was talking about the drought.

7 Paragraph 4 is mostly about—

Ⓐ Emilio's family.

Ⓑ why Emilio feels lonely.

Ⓒ the foggy eucalyptus woods.

Ⓓ Emilio's old house in New Mexico.

8 Emilio hurried back to the house to get a plastic jar so he could—

Ⓕ capture and save some of the tadpoles.

Ⓖ give the tadpoles more water.

Ⓗ examine the tadpoles more closely.

Ⓘ show his parents the tadpoles.

9 Read this sentence from paragraph 6.

A carpet of fallen leaves shaped like feathers cushioned his steps as he jogged down the path to the nearby creek.

Which of the following is an example of figurative language in the sentence?

Ⓐ A carpet of fallen leaves shaped like feathers

Ⓑ cushioned his steps

Ⓒ as he jogged

Ⓓ the path to the nearby creek

10 What does the word **cushioned** mean in paragraph 6?

Ⓕ padded

Ⓖ scratched

Ⓗ marked

Ⓘ showed

GO ON

Practice Reading Test 7—Emilio's Tadpoles

11 If all of the water evaporated from the streambed, the tadpoles would—

(A) find a new water source.

(B) probably die.

(C) burrow underground.

(D) look for food.

12 At the end of the story, Emilio—

(F) missed his old friends even more.

(G) no longer felt sorry for himself.

(H) was afraid of the foggy eucalyptus woods.

(J) felt bored.

13 Which sentence belongs in the box to show the sequence of events in the story?

Emilio's family moves to California.

↓

↓

Emilio decides to stop feeling sorry for himself.

↓

Emilio discovers tadpoles in stagnant pools.

(A) Emilio runs to his house for a plastic jar.

(B) Emilio, Carlos, and Jose play air hockey.

(C) Emilio misses his friends.

(D) Emilio decides to help the tadpoles.

14 Which detail from the story belongs in the concept web below?

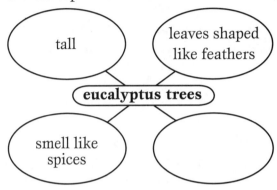

(F) only grow in cold, arctic climates

(G) have smooth brown bark

(H) keep leaves year round

(J) have shaggy bark

15 How did Emilio know that the animals he discovered in the stagnant pools were tadpoles?

(A) Only tadpoles live in pools.

(B) A few of the swimmers had back legs.

(C) They were tiny and dark-colored.

(D) B and C

16 SHORT ANSWER: Answer the following question on a separate sheet of paper. Use complete sentences.

What do you think happened next? Write an ending for this story.

Directions: Read the article. Then answer questions 1 through 12.

The Midnight Ride

(1)   Late one night in 1775, a man named Paul Revere set out on a journey from Boston that would make history. At that time, King George III of Great Britain ruled the American colonies. He forced the colonists to pay taxes and follow his rules. They wanted to set up their own government and make their own rules. This made King George very angry. He ordered British soldiers to arrest the rebels and take control of the city of Boston.

(2)   Paul Revere and many other colonists were ready to fight against the British king's army. They called themselves minutemen because they had to be ready to fight at a moment's notice. The colonists had found out that the British soldiers were going to arrest rebel leaders Samuel Adams and John Hancock. On the night of April 18, 1775, Paul Revere was asked to ride to Lexington, Massachusetts, to warn Adams and Hancock that the British soldiers were coming to arrest them.

(3)   Paul already knew that the British would march toward Lexington and Concord. But he didn't know whether they would come by land or across the water. When he found out, Paul would have a man named Robert Newman hang lanterns in the tower of Boston's Old North Church. One lantern would mean that the British were coming by land. Two lanterns would mean they were coming by water. This would warn others of the route that the soldiers were taking.

(4)   Word finally came from the American spies—the British were coming by water. Immediately, Paul ordered two lanterns to be hung in the church tower. He rowed across the Charles River and then rode fast into the night on a waiting horse. Paul knew how important it was to warn Adams, Hancock, and the minutemen. The British army had more men and more guns than the colonists. The minutemen would have to surprise them. Paul and two other men rode into Lexington, warning people as they went. But as they rode out of town, the British captured them. Paul did not escape. Fortunately, the two other riders did. They made it to Concord and warned the minutemen to be ready to fight.

(5)   Soon the British army reached Concord. They had no idea that the minutemen were waiting. Because of the bravery of Paul Revere and others, the minutemen won their first fight—the American Revolution had begun. Someday, there would be freedom.

GO ON ➡

Practice Reading Test 8—The Midnight Ride

1   Another title for this article might be—

    Ⓐ "Paul Revere's Famous Ride"

    Ⓑ "Minutemen"

    Ⓒ "King George III"

    Ⓓ "Colonial Times"

2   Read this sentence from paragraph 4.

Immediately, Paul ordered that two lanterns be hung in the church tower.

What does the word **immediately** mean?

    Ⓕ without delay

    Ⓖ recently

    Ⓗ slowly

    Ⓙ carefully

3   Because the British soldiers were planning to arrest Hancock and Adams,—

    Ⓐ Paul Revere formed an army.

    Ⓑ Paul Revere hid them.

    Ⓒ Paul Revere was asked to warn them.

    Ⓓ Paul Revere rode to Boston.

4   Read this sentence from paragraph 1.

He ordered British soldiers to arrest the rebels and take control of the city of Boston.

What does the word **ordered** mean?

    Ⓕ the sequence of things

    Ⓖ a state of peace

    Ⓗ to arrange

    Ⓙ commanded

5   The colonists were _____ to fight for their freedom.

    Ⓐ afraid

    Ⓑ determined

    Ⓒ too weak

    Ⓓ too poor

6   Who were the American spies?

    Ⓕ people who wrote stories about the British

    Ⓖ people who tried to get secret information about the British

    Ⓗ people who secretly worked for the British

    Ⓙ people the colonists couldn't trust

GO ON ➡

7 One lantern hung in the church tower was the signal that the British were coming by ____.

    Ⓐ land

    Ⓑ water

    Ⓒ horses

    Ⓓ ships

8 Choose the correct sentence to put in the box to complete the story summary below.

> 1. King George III wanted to keep his control over the colonies.

> 2. The rebels found out that the British were coming to arrest their leaders.

> 3.

> 4. Paul Revere was captured by the British as he rode out of Lexington.

    Ⓕ Paul Revere organized a group of soldiers called minutemen.

    Ⓖ The minutemen won the fight.

    Ⓗ Paul Revere was sent to warn Hancock and Adams.

    Ⓙ The minutemen were ready to fight in Concord.

9 When does this story take place?

    Ⓐ in the present

    Ⓑ in colonial times

    Ⓒ in the 1900s

    Ⓓ in the future

10 Paul Revere made history because—

    Ⓕ he ordered two lanterns to be hung in the church tower.

    Ⓖ he was brave to make the journey.

    Ⓗ he helped the minutemen win their first fight against the British.

    Ⓙ he captured British soldiers.

11 Which book would give you more information about Paul Revere?

    Ⓐ *Famous American Women*

    Ⓑ *Famous Inventors*

    Ⓒ *Famous American Colonists*

    Ⓓ *American Presidents*

12 Which word correctly completes the following sentence?

The minutemen needed ____ surprise the British army.

    Ⓕ two   Ⓗ too

    Ⓖ to   Ⓙ tow

Directions: Read the article. Then answer questions 1 through 13.

SAGUARO CACTUS

(1) In the hot, dry Arizona desert grows a cactus that can live as long as 200 years. Its name is the saguaro. A saguaro cactus grows very slowly. But as it does, it becomes a home and a source of food for many desert animals.

(2) The saguaro cactus begins its life as a tiny black seed. There may be over 2,000 seeds in one bright red saguaro fruit! Only a few seeds ever sprout and grow. First, a rare rain must give it moisture. Then the seed swells up, splits its shell, and sends a root down into the desert soil. The roots don't grow very deep, but they produce a stem that will grow tall and strong over the years.

(3) It doesn't rain often in the desert, so the little stem grows slowly. The saguaro often grows in the shelter of another shrub or tree. This tree is called a "nurse plant" because it helps to protect the little cactus with shade and moisture. After one year, the saguaro may only be half an inch high. After 10 years, it may still be fewer than 6 inches (15 centimeters) tall. When it is 50 years old, the original stem—now the plant's trunk—is about 15 feet (4.5 meters) tall. It can take over 50 years for the saguaro cactus to grow its first branches, which are called arms. Like the trunk, its arms are moist and prickly. How prickly are they? The saguaro's spines are two inches long and grow in clusters. Over the next 50 years, the saguaro cactus may grow as tall as 35 feet (10.5 meters).

(4) When it rains, the saguaro's trunk and arms expand and absorb moisture like a sponge. Because of the cactus's moist skin, many animals like to make the cactus their homes. Gila woodpeckers carve out deep nests in the sides of saguaro stems and lay their eggs. After the eggs hatch, the baby woodpeckers eat the insects that live on the cactus. Mice, hawks, and owls may also use the vacant nests built by the woodpeckers.

(5) The mature saguaro cactus produces beautiful white flowers with yellow centers. These three-inch-wide flowers have sweet nectar that birds, bats, and insects drink. The saguaro cactus has been named the state flower of Arizona.

(6) If the flower has been pollinated, a sweet, juicy, green fruit begins to form. Many desert animals like to eat both the fruit and its seeds. The animals help to spread the seeds from the fruit on the ground. There they stay, waiting for rain so they can sprout and grow into new saguaro cactuses.

GO ON →

Practice Reading Test 9—Saguaro Cactus

1 Paragraph 1 says that the saguaro cactus grows very slowly. What is a synonym for the word **slowly**?

Ⓐ quickly

Ⓑ gradually

Ⓒ prickly

Ⓓ rarely

2 According to the article, a full-grown cactus may grow as tall as _____.

Ⓕ 15 centimeters

Ⓖ 15 feet

Ⓗ 4.5 meters

Ⓙ 35 feet

3 Read the following sentence from paragraph 2.

First, a rare rain must give it moisture.

What does the word **moisture** mean?

Ⓐ coolness

Ⓑ nutrients

Ⓒ wetness

Ⓓ air

4 This article is _____.

Ⓕ fiction

Ⓖ nonfiction

Ⓗ drama

Ⓙ poetry

5 Read the following sentence from paragraph 3.

When it is 50 years old, the original stem—now the plant's trunk—is about 15 feet (4.5 meters) tall.

What does the word **original** mean?

Ⓐ limited

Ⓑ the first

Ⓒ previous

Ⓓ mature

6 This article was written to—

Ⓕ explain how to grow saguaro cactuses.

Ⓖ tell the reader about the saguaro cactus.

Ⓗ persuade the reader to visit the desert in Arizona.

Ⓙ describe desert animals.

7 Many desert animals make their homes in the saguaro cactus because—

Ⓐ there are no other plants in the desert.

Ⓑ it is the largest plant in the desert.

Ⓒ it provides food and protection for animals.

Ⓓ it is the prettiest plant in the desert.

8 The saguaro cactus grows very slowly because—

Ⓕ it doesn't rain often in the desert.

Ⓖ so many animals make the cactus their homes.

Ⓗ the soil in the desert is hard.

Ⓙ it has a thick, tough skin.

9 Which of the following is not a detail from the story?

Ⓐ The saguaro cactus can live 200 years or more.

Ⓑ Woodpeckers build nests in the side of the cactus.

Ⓒ Bats make the saguaro cactus their home.

Ⓓ Flowers grow on the mature saguaro cactus.

10 How is the cactus able to survive in the desert climate?

Ⓕ The cactus grows quickly because of the large amount of rainfall in the desert.

Ⓖ The cactus absorbs and stores water when it rains.

Ⓗ The animals that make the cactus their home provide moisture.

Ⓙ The cactus's roots grow deep to find water underground.

11 Which of the following phrases belongs in the box to complete the cactus life cycle?

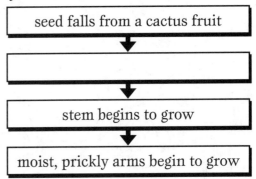

```
┌─────────────────────────────────┐
│   seed falls from a cactus fruit │
└─────────────────────────────────┘
                 ↓
┌─────────────────────────────────┐
│                                 │
└─────────────────────────────────┘
                 ↓
┌─────────────────────────────────┐
│       stem begins to grow       │
└─────────────────────────────────┘
                 ↓
┌─────────────────────────────────┐
│ moist, prickly arms begin to grow│
└─────────────────────────────────┘
```

Ⓐ flowers begin to grow

Ⓑ flowers become juicy, green fruit

Ⓒ root grows from the seed into the soil

Ⓓ it provides a home for many animals

12 Which phrase from the article is an example of a simile?

Ⓕ beautiful white flowers with yellow centers

Ⓖ the cactus's moist skin

Ⓗ absorb moisture like a sponge

Ⓙ a sweet, juicy, green fruit

13 SHORT ANSWER: Answer the following question on a separate sheet of paper. Use complete sentences.

Write a paragraph summarizing the life cycle of the saguaro cactus. Use details from the article in your paragraph.

STOP

Directions: Read the story. Then answer questions 1 through 15.

A Field Trip to the Recycling Center

(1) Clayton's class was getting ready to go on a field trip. Clayton's teacher, Mr. Porter, told the class that they would be visiting a recycling center. The students talked about different materials that could be recycled. They would visit a center that recycled plastic. Mr. Porter wanted the students to talk about recycling plastic before the field trip. For homework, he asked them to list all of the things they could think of that were made of plastic.

(2) The next day, the students shared their lists. They learned that we use plastic every day. Many things in our homes—toys, dishes, shoes, bags, and containers—are made from plastics. Scientists have worked hard over the years to make plastics strong. Plastic is not a natural material. It does not easily decompose back into the soil. Mr. Porter explained that we must be careful about how we throw away plastic materials. Plastic containers and bags can pollute our beaches and hurt animals. The limited space in our landfills and garbage dumps also needs to be considered.

(3) "One thing we all can do is recycle our plastic containers," he said. "Some grocery stores ask customers if they want paper or plastic bags. Plastic grocery bags can be used for other things, too. Plastic bags can be burned because they do not give off poisonous fumes. Other plastics make the air toxic, or poisonous, when they are burned."

(4) Then Mr. Porter passed around some plastic containers for the students to look at. "When you are shopping," he said, "look at the bottom of each plastic container you buy. If it has a recycle symbol with a number on it, you know it can be recycled."

(5) Clayton looked at the plastic jug Mr. Porter gave him. It had the recycle symbol and the number 5 on the bottom. Mr. Porter explained that their community did not recycle number 5 plastics. "Can you think of another way to recycle that container?" he asked.

Practice Reading Test 10—A Field Trip to the Recycling Center

(6) Clayton thought for a moment. Then he said, "I could use it for something else instead of just throwing it away. This jug has a wide opening and it has a lid. I could put Buster's bone-shaped treats in it to keep them fresh."

(7) "That's right," Mr. Porter agreed. "Sharing toys and hand-me-downs is another great way to recycle. When you're done playing with a plastic toy, try to think of someone else who could use it. Do you have a younger neighbor or a cousin who might like what you have outgrown? Someone else might enjoy your old things."

(8) Finally, it was time to visit the recycling center. Clayton and his classmates learned that many recycling centers sell used plastic to companies. These companies process the plastic and make new things. Some companies make park benches out of recycled plastic. Plastic also can be used to make carpets, fabric, and stuffing for ski jackets. Recycled plastic can become support structures for walkways, decks, and even some buildings. These plastic products can be made in different colors and will last for a long time. By the end of the trip, the students agreed that it is important to find ways to recycle plastic. Mr. Porter challenged them to be creative and to keep thinking of new ways to reuse their plastic things.

1 Read this sentence from paragraph 1.

The students talked about different materials that could be recycled.

What does the word **materials** mean in this sentence?

Ⓐ fabric or cloth

Ⓑ tools needed to perform a task

Ⓒ information found in books or research

Ⓓ the substance used to make things

2 Choose the word in which the root word is underlined.

Ⓕ <u>rent</u>

Ⓖ re<u>use</u>

Ⓗ re<u>ward</u>

Ⓙ <u>recycle</u>

3 Read this sentence from paragraph 2.

Scientists have worked hard over the years to make plastics strong.

What does the word **strong** mean?

Ⓐ extreme

Ⓑ effective

Ⓒ sturdy

Ⓓ an intense odor

Practice Reading Test 10—A Field Trip to the Recycling Center

4   Which of the following statements is a fact?

  Ⓕ You should not use plastic products.

  Ⓖ Plastics are the best materials for toys.

  Ⓗ Some plastic things can be made into new items.

  Ⓙ Things made from recycled plastic are ugly.

5   Who is Buster?

  Ⓐ Clayton's classmate

  Ⓑ Clayton's brother

  Ⓒ Clayton's dog

  Ⓓ Clayton's cat

6   What will students in Clayton's class probably do after their visit to the recycling center?

  Ⓕ convince the principal to use plastic plates and dishes in the cafeteria

  Ⓖ go out and buy new plastic toys

  Ⓗ tell their families and friends how important it is to recycle plastic

  Ⓙ use only recycled products

7   This story mostly takes place—

  Ⓐ at the recycling center.

  Ⓑ at school.

  Ⓒ at Clayton's house.

  Ⓓ at the landfill.

8   Which phrase best describes Clayton's attitude toward recycling?

  Ⓕ not at all interested in learning about recycling

  Ⓖ very interested in learning about recycling

  Ⓗ upset that the class was going to the recycling center

  Ⓙ angry with people who do not recycle

9   One way plastics are affecting our landfills and garbage dumps is—

  Ⓐ plastics give off toxic fumes.

  Ⓑ plastics can pollute our beaches.

  Ⓒ plastics do not easily decompose.

  Ⓓ plastics smell bad.

10   Which of the following phrases belongs in the concept web?

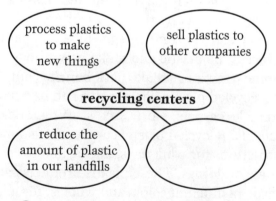

  Ⓕ make the air toxic when burned

  Ⓖ help people reuse plastics

  Ⓗ share toys and hand-me-downs

  Ⓙ pollute our beaches

GO ON

Practice Reading Test 10—A Field Trip to the Recycling Center

11   Read this sentence from paragraph 2.

Plastic containers and bags can pollute our beaches and hurt animals.

What does the word **pollute** mean?

Ⓐ to damage with harmful materials

Ⓑ to make bad choices

Ⓒ to keep the same

Ⓓ to move forward

12   The author probably wrote this article to—

Ⓕ teach the reader how to stop pollution.

Ⓖ convince the reader not to use plastic containers.

Ⓗ teach the reader why it is important to recycle.

Ⓙ teach the reader about landfills.

13   According to the story, which of the following is NOT something made from recycled plastic?

Ⓐ carpets

Ⓑ park benches

Ⓒ stuffing for ski jackets

Ⓓ paper grocery bags

14   Which sentence belongs in the box to show the sequence of events in the story?

Clayton's class shared their lists of the plastic things they use every day.

↓

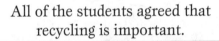

↓

All of the students agreed that recycling is important.

↓

Ⓕ Mr. Porter assigned homework.

Ⓖ Clayton's class visited the recycling center.

Ⓗ Mr. Porter told Clayton's class they would be visiting a recycling center.

Ⓙ none of the above

15   Read this sentence about plastic from paragraph 2.

It does not easily decompose back into the soil.

What is a synonym for the word **decompose**?

Ⓐ relax

Ⓑ decay

Ⓒ decrease

Ⓓ sink

Directions: Read the story. Then answer questions 1 through 15.

Stained Light

(1) Alexis and Emma were working together on a project for world history. Their class was studying the Middle Ages. There were many interesting topics. The problem was that most of the interesting subjects had already been chosen. Some of the students were doing reports about the Black Death, knights, and the Crusades. Others were learning about tapestries, costumes, and handwritten books.

(2) "Maybe we should do our report on art or music," Alexis suggested.

(3) "Or we could study the kinds of homes they built," said Emma. She thought for a moment. "But Ms. Sinclair talked about those topics in class. Everybody has already heard about them. We need to do something different!"

(4) The next Saturday they met at the library and looked at the library's catalog on the computer. The library had lots of books about the Middle Ages. Alexis scrolled down through the titles. She stopped suddenly and pointed to a book about Gothic cathedrals. "Last month I saw a video about a cathedral built near Paris in the 12th century," she said. "It was called the Abbey of Saint-Denis, and everybody in the town helped build it. Some men started working on the cathedral when they were young. They worked on it their whole lives."

(5) "There was a book about that, too," said Emma. "I read it last year. Let's find some books about cathedrals."

(6) The girls printed out a list of books and found the right section in the library. Some of the books were checked out, but there were four left on the shelf. Alexis and Emma each took two. They carried them to a quiet study table and started to look at the pictures. Alexis found a picture of a beautiful stained-glass window in a large cathedral.

GO ON ➡

Practice Reading Test 11—Stained Light

(7) "Look," she whispered. Together the girls read that Gothic cathedrals were made of stone and were very tall. They needed big windows to bring light into the building. Artists designed the windows using pieces of colored or stained glass. When light shone through the windows, the people inside the cathedral could see glowing pictures or designs of color in the glass. These buildings became an important part of medieval life.

(8) "This is it!" Alexis said. "Maybe we can even make a model to go with our report!" As the girls looked at other beautiful photographs of cathedrals, they were excited to start their project on stained-glass windows.

1 Read this sentence from paragraph 1.

Others were learning about tapestries, costumes, and handwritten books.

What does the word **tapestries** mean?

- Ⓐ embroidered fabrics
- Ⓑ buildings
- Ⓒ dances
- Ⓓ parties

2 Read this sentence from paragraph 7.

When light shone through the windows, the people inside the cathedral could see glowing pictures or designs of color in the glass.

Which word means the same as **designs**?

- Ⓕ drawings
- Ⓖ patterns
- Ⓗ plans
- Ⓙ windows

3 This story is _____.

- Ⓐ historical fiction
- Ⓑ science fiction
- Ⓒ nonfiction
- Ⓓ fiction

4 Read these sentences from paragraph 6 in the story.

Some of the books were checked out, but there were four left on the shelf. Alexis and Emma each took two. They carried them to a quiet study table and started to look at the pictures.

Which part of the story does this passage tell about?

Ⓐ characters

Ⓑ speaker or narrator

Ⓒ plot

Ⓓ resolution

5 What are the girls most likely to create for their project?

Ⓐ a model of a castle made from cardboard

Ⓑ a model of a cathedral out of clay

Ⓒ a stained-glass window using tissue and construction paper

Ⓓ a costume with beads and jewels

6 Which of the following statements is a fact?

Ⓐ Stained-glass windows are beautiful.

Ⓑ Cathedrals are interesting to study.

Ⓒ Cathedrals are tall buildings.

Ⓓ The most exciting period in history is the Middle Ages.

7 Gothic cathedrals were made of—

Ⓐ bricks.

Ⓑ cement.

Ⓒ stone.

Ⓓ wood.

8 Read this summary of the first part of the story.

Alexis and Emma wanted to do their world history project on a topic that no other student had chosen. They met at the library to find an interesting subject.

Which of the following sentences completes the summary above?

Ⓐ The girls found many different book titles listed under the Middle Ages.

Ⓑ Alexis saw a video about building a cathedral.

Ⓒ Ms. Sinclair talked about art in the Middle Ages.

Ⓓ Emma read a book about the Abbey of Saint-Denis.

9 Which word from the story contains a suffix?

Ⓐ section

Ⓑ library

Ⓒ model

Ⓓ stained

GO ON

Practice Reading Test 11—Stained Light

10 Paragraph 7 is mostly about—

⒡ buildings of the Middle Ages.

⒢ the people that built cathedrals.

⒣ the stained-glass windows in cathedrals.

⒥ the artists who designed the windows.

11 Which of the following statements is an opinion?

Ⓐ Alexis and Emma were studying the Middle Ages in school.

Ⓑ Alexis and Emma visited the library to do research.

Ⓒ Alexis and Emma found pictures of stained glass windows.

Ⓓ Alexis and Emma chose an exciting topic to study.

12 The girls went to the library because they—

⒡ had books to return.

⒢ wanted to find some books about cathedrals.

⒣ wanted to ask the librarian for an idea.

⒥ wanted to find a topic that was different.

13 Choose the correct word to complete this sentence.

Alexis and Emma wanted to ____ a report on stained-glass windows.

Ⓐ rite   Ⓒ right

Ⓑ write   Ⓓ white

14 Most of the story takes place—

⒡ at the library.

⒢ at Alexis's house.

⒣ on the playground.

⒥ in Ms. Sinclair's classroom.

15 Read the dictionary entry below.

section ('sek-shən)

n **1.** a piece of land one square mile in area   *n* **2.** a segment of fruit   *n* **3.** a distinct part of something   *v* **4.** to cut into parts

Which meaning BEST describes the word **section** as used in paragraph 6?

Ⓐ definition 1

Ⓑ definition 2

Ⓒ definition 3

Ⓓ definition 4

STOP

Directions: Read the story. Then answer questions 1 through 15.

A Class Trip to the Zoo

(1)   Dylan was excited. His class had been studying animals and their habitats. Now they were taking a field trip to the city zoo. Dylan's teacher, Mr. Sullivan, had explained that a habitat is a place where an animal lives. He said each living thing must adapt to its environment in order to survive. Mr. Sullivan told the students to think about an animal that they would like to study. After the trip, each student could choose one animal and write a report on it.

(2)   The day of the class trip finally came. When Dylan's class arrived at the zoo, they found that it was divided into sections. Each section was a different kind of habitat. The first section they visited was the mountain habitat. The students saw bears and golden eagles. The habitat also contained deer, elk, sheep, and mountain goats. Dylan learned that not many animals lived high up in the mountains. Most animals couldn't survive the harsh conditions. There were also dangers such as steep slopes, strong winds, and falling rocks. Not many plants survive in the mountain habitat, either.

(3)   The class then visited the forest habitat. They saw raccoons, wild boars, and porcupines. Forest hunters included wolves, bobcats, and owls. Some animals from the mountain habitat lived in the forest, too. Mr. Sullivan told the students that some forest habitats are shrinking. When a forest is destroyed to build homes or stores, the forest animals have to find new homes.

(4)   Next, the students went to the grasslands section. The zoo guide told them that the grasslands are also called savannas. Many of the interesting animals in this section were from Africa. The students saw giraffes, lions, elephants, and zebras. There were even some hippopotamuses. Animals who live in the grasslands like the warm climate. Mr. Sullivan told the students that this was his favorite habitat to study.

(5)   But Dylan's favorite section was next—the tropical rainforest. The rainforest habitat was warm and moist. It had many trees and plants and many different types of animals. Dylan saw jaguars and crocodiles. He heard the noisy toucans and parrots. At last they came to the gorillas and chimpanzees. The guide explained that gorillas and chimpanzees are called primates because they have very complex brains, like humans. Gorillas and chimpanzees are among the most intelligent of all animals. They can think, and they use tools with their hands. Although the gorillas were bigger, Dylan especially liked watching the chimpanzees. He thought they looked the most like humans. Some of the chimpanzees were even using sticks to get honey from a honeycomb.

(6)   On the way back to school, Dylan thought about all the animals he had seen. He knew which animal he wanted to write his report about, and he couldn't wait to get started!

1 Dylan and his classmates must decide—

  (A) which part of the zoo is their favorite.

  (B) which animals they would like to study.

  (C) where to go for a class trip.

  (D) which forest animals they like the best.

2 Read this sentence from paragraph 1.

He said that each living thing must adapt to its environment in order to survive.

What does the word **adapt** mean?

  (F) adjust

  (G) live

  (H) invade

  (J) travel

3 The author's purpose for writing this story was to—

  (A) tell about Dylan's class.

  (B) explain how animals survive in harsh conditions.

  (C) tell about different animal habitats.

  (D) explain how a class trip is organized.

Practice Reading Test 12—A Class Trip to the Zoo

4 The author organized this story by—

    Ⓕ comparing land animals with water animals.

    Ⓖ writing about a specific species in each paragraph.

    Ⓗ writing about animals found in different countries.

    Ⓙ describing each habitat and the animals that live there.

5 In which section of the zoo did Dylan see the bobcats?

    Ⓐ the forest habitat

    Ⓑ the savanna habitat

    Ⓒ the mountain habitat

    Ⓓ the tropical rainforest habitat

6 Which sentence from the story shows that Dylan is eager to begin his report?

    Ⓕ When they returned from the trip, the students would be writing reports on their favorite animals.

    Ⓖ On the way back to school, Dylan thought about all the animals he had seen.

    Ⓗ He knew which animal he wanted to write his report about, and he couldn't wait to get started!

    Ⓙ Although the gorillas were bigger, Dylan really liked watching the chimpanzees.

7 Read the following sentence from paragraph 4 and the dictionary entry below.

The zoo guide told them that the grasslands are also called savannas.

guide ('gīd)
n **1.** a manual
n **2.** someone who supervises a tour
v **3.** to steer or direct
v **4.** to lead someone in the right direction

Which meaning BEST describes the word **guide** as used in the sentence above?

    Ⓐ definition 1

    Ⓑ definition 2

    Ⓒ definition 3

    Ⓓ definition 4

8 What are grasslands sometimes called?

    Ⓕ forests

    Ⓖ deserts

    Ⓗ savannas

    Ⓙ wild lands

9 Where does most of the story take place?

    Ⓐ in Dylan's classroom

    Ⓑ at the zoo

    Ⓒ in the rainforest habitat

    Ⓓ at the library

GO ON ➡

Practice Reading Test 12—A Class Trip to the Zoo

10   What will Dylan most likely write his report on?

     (F)   gorillas

     (G)   chimpanzees

     (H)   mountain goats

     (J)   giraffes

11   Which statement is an opinion?

     (A)   Gorillas are bigger than chimpanzees.

     (B)   The rainforest habitat is warm and moist.

     (C)   Living things must adapt to their environment in order to survive.

     (D)   The grasslands habitat is the most interesting habitat to study.

12   Which sentence BEST describes how Dylan felt at the end of the story?

     (F)   Dylan wanted to be a tour guide at the zoo.

     (G)   Dylan was excited about what he had learned at the zoo.

     (H)   Dylan was upset because some forests were being destroyed.

     (J)   Dylan was tired after such a long day.

13   Choose the word from the article with the underlined suffix.

     (A)   rainfor<u>est</u>

     (B)   bigg<u>est</u>

     (C)   b<u>est</u>

     (D)   mo<u>ist</u>

14   What does the story say is one effect of the destruction of forest habitats?

     (F)   Many forest animals will become extinct.

     (G)   Grassland habitats will grow larger.

     (H)   The forest animals must find new homes.

     (J)   More zoos will be built to provide forest habitats.

15   Read this sentence from paragraph 2.

Most animals couldn't survive the harsh conditions.

Which word is a synonym for the word **harsh** as it is used in the sentence?

     (A)   severe

     (B)   scratchy

     (C)   angry

     (D)   painful

STOP

Directions: Read the story. Then answer questions 1 through 12.

Another Use for Seeds

(1) Karsen got off the school bus, still puzzled by her teacher's art assignment. Just a few hours ago, she was sitting in Ms. Pennington's class listening to her teacher explain the next assignment. "I want each of you to 'artistically present' your own house," she had said. Karsen immediately thought of her boxes of markers, crayons, colored pencils, and watercolors. She could make a very artistic presentation with the huge range of colors from which she could choose. This project would be a breeze! "But," Ms. Pennington had continued, "you may not use any pencils, crayons, paints, or markers." Karsen and her classmates were stunned. This would be impossible. How could they draw without any materials?

(2) When several students tried to ask questions, Ms. Pennington had just smiled. "You should all just use your imaginations," she said. Then class ended and it was time to go to lunch. Karsen, Leah, and Sonya sat at their favorite table and talked about the strange art assignment.

(3) "My father's an architect," Leah said. "I'm going to ask him for help."

(4) Sonya thought for a second. "Hey, my grandmother is always doing crafts. Maybe she'll have some ideas."

(5) When Karsen arrived home, there was just time to grab her jacket to go to her brother Ian's soccer game. Karsen's dad planned to meet them there. While they were waiting for the coin toss to start the game, Karsen asked her mom for a snack. "I think the snack stand is open," said her mom, pointing to a building next to the bleachers.

(6) Karsen bought a drink and a package of sunflower seeds and went back to join her mother. Soon her dad arrived. As they watched the game, they talked about school. Karsen told her parents about the weird art assignment. "I don't know what I'm going to do!" she said.

Practice Reading Test 13—Another Use for Seeds

(7) Karsen barely watched the game. She just couldn't come up with any ideas for her art project. As she thought, she began playing with her empty sunflower seed shells, placing them in rows and circles on the seat beside her. Suddenly, she realized that the seeds could create a picture. Better yet, seeds come in different colors. She could make a mosaic using seeds! Karsen excitedly began to plan her project. She would use pumpkin seeds for the white painted wood on their house and corn seeds for the yellow shutters. Her mind was racing. Using seeds was an original idea. Now the project would be fun to do.

(8) Later that evening, Karsen's father sat down to help her with the project. He told her that she was welcome to use the packets of last year's garden seeds stored in the garage. Karsen ran to get the seeds, then found some paper and glue. She was ready to begin working on her "artistic presentation."

1 Read this sentence from paragraph 1.

> **"I want each of you to 'artistically present' your own house," she had said.**

What does the word **present** mean in this sentence?

Ⓐ to give something to someone in a formal manner

Ⓑ to show or display something in a particular way

Ⓒ a gift or offering

Ⓓ taking place or existing now

2 In paragraph 3, Leah says her father is an **architect**. What does the word **architect** mean?

Ⓕ a person who designs buildings

Ⓖ a person who builds arches

Ⓗ an artist

Ⓙ a person who sells artwork

3 After school, Karsen went to her brother's _____ game.

Ⓐ baseball   Ⓒ soccer

Ⓑ football   Ⓓ hockey

4 Karsen thought the art assignment would be _____ until her teacher explained it.

Ⓕ easy   Ⓗ difficult

Ⓖ boring   Ⓙ fun

GO ON

Practice Reading Test 13—Another Use for Seeds

5 Karsen's teacher told the students not to use pencils, crayons, markers, or paints because—

   Ⓐ she wanted the students to be creative.

   Ⓑ she wanted the art to be in black and white.

   Ⓒ she didn't want the students to make a mess.

   Ⓓ she wanted to make the assignment difficult for them.

6 Which of the following is a fact?

   Ⓕ The art assignment was weird.

   Ⓖ Sunflower seeds taste good.

   Ⓗ Seeds come in different colors.

   Ⓙ Karsen's project would be the best one in the class.

7 Because Ms. Pennington told the students they couldn't use pencils, crayons, markers, or paints—

   Ⓐ the students were confused.

   Ⓑ the students were angry.

   Ⓒ the students were excited.

   Ⓓ the students were eager to get started.

8 In paragraph 7, Karsen thinks using seeds is an **original** idea. What does the word **original** mean?

   Ⓕ exceptional   Ⓗ outstanding

   Ⓖ wonderful   Ⓙ creative

9 Karsen got the idea to make a seed mosaic from—

   Ⓐ her father.

   Ⓑ her mother.

   Ⓒ playing with sunflower seeds.

   Ⓓ a book about art.

10 Paragraph 5 is mostly about—

   Ⓕ Karsen's teacher explaining the assignment.

   Ⓖ Karsen and her friends talking about the assignment.

   Ⓗ Karsen at her brother's game.

   Ⓙ Karsen and her friends eating lunch.

11 Which event happened last?

   Ⓐ Ms. Pennington gave the students an art assignment.

   Ⓑ Karsen went to her brother's soccer game.

   Ⓒ Karsen discovered she could make a picture using seeds.

   Ⓓ Karsen and her dad began to work on the project.

12 What else might Karsen use to complete her seed mosaic?

   Ⓕ grass

   Ⓖ flower petals

   Ⓗ songbird food

   Ⓙ pebbles

Directions: Read the article. Then answer questions 1 through 12.

Amelia Earhart

(1) Amelia Earhart was born in 1897. She and her younger sister Muriel grew up in Atchison, Kansas. Back in those days, people thought girls and women should behave differently from boys and men. But Amelia and Muriel were tomboys. They wore loose-fitting pants called bloomers instead of dresses. They loved to climb trees, play football, and go fishing with their father. Amelia's grandmother didn't approve of their behavior. She thought they should act like young ladies.

(2) Even as a young child, Amelia loved adventure. She liked to discover new things. Her family once went to a fair, and she saw a roller coaster for the first time. Amelia's mother wouldn't let her ride it because she thought it was too dangerous. But that didn't stop Amelia. She built her own roller coaster using some long, old boards and a crate. She nailed one end of the boards to the roof of a tool shed and rested the other end on the ground to make a track. Then she climbed into the crate at the top of the track and raced to the bottom.

(3) Amelia was just six years old when the Wright brothers flew the first plane. Many people were excited about the new flying machines. But young Amelia wasn't very impressed with them. When she was 11 years old, she and her family went to the Iowa State Fair where Amelia first saw an airplane. "That's not at all interesting," Amelia said. "It's just a thing made of rusty wire and wood."

(4) As she was growing up, Amelia dreamed about what she would be when she was older. Amelia wanted to prove that women could do great things. She kept a scrapbook about women with unusual careers. But even then, she never thought about being a pilot. After high school, Amelia worked as a nurse's aide in Toronto, Canada. One day she went to an air show. Amelia watched as the pilots performed daring stunts. For the first time, she was interested. She couldn't stop thinking about what it would be like to fly in an airplane. A few years later, in 1920, she took her first airplane ride. As soon as the plane was in the air, Amelia knew she wanted to be a pilot.

(5) Amelia went to Los Angeles, California, where she met Neta Snook. Neta was a pilot and a flying instructor. Those were unusual jobs for women back in those days. Neta agreed to give Amelia flying lessons. Amelia took her first lesson in 1921 and got a job at a local phone company to pay for the lessons. She learned fast and loved to be in the air. That summer, she bought her first plane. It was bright yellow, and she called it "The Canary." Within a year, Amelia had set her first record. She flew to a height of 14,000 feet (4,300 meters), a new altitude record for women pilots. But that was just the beginning.

(6) Amelia went on to set many records. By the time she was 26 years old, Amelia became the first woman to be a licensed pilot. In 1928, two male pilots invited Amelia to join them on a flight across the Atlantic. They flew from Canada to Wales. Amelia was famous! She was the first woman to fly across the Atlantic Ocean. Four years later, Amelia flew across the Atlantic Ocean again. This time, she flew alone.

(7) People loved Amelia's adventurous spirit. She won many awards for her accomplishments and even wrote a book about one of her flights. But Amelia still wasn't finished breaking records. She wanted to fly around the world—a journey of 29,000 miles (46,700 kilometers). On June 1, 1937, she and Fred Noonan, her navigator, took off from Miami, Florida. They flew eastward and visited many countries. By late June, they had reached New Guinea in the southwest Pacific Ocean. They had already flown 22,000 miles (35,400 kilometers). On July 2, Amelia and Fred left New Guinea. It was shortly after noon. Their next goal was tiny Howland Island, 2,500 miles (4,000 kilometers) away in the middle of the Pacific. But they never got there. Lost and low on fuel, Fred and Amelia disappeared on July 3. Many people searched the waters and islands of the South Pacific for them. But no one found a clue. Amelia Earhart and Fred Noonan were never seen again.

(8) What happened to Amelia Earhart? Her death remains a mystery to this day. But we can learn a lot from the way she lived. Amelia continues to inspire us with her courage and love for learning new things.

GO ON

Practice Reading Test 14—Amelia Earhart

1 Read these sentences from paragraph 1.

But Amelia and Muriel were tomboys. They wore loose-fitting pants called bloomers instead of dresses.

What does the word **tomboy** mean?

Ⓐ a girl who behaves in a boyish manner

Ⓑ a boy who likes to climb trees

Ⓒ a child who likes airplanes

Ⓓ an unruly child

2 As Amelia was growing up, she—

Ⓕ always dreamed of being a pilot.

Ⓖ admired the Wright brothers.

Ⓗ studied women with unusual careers.

Ⓙ wanted to play football.

3 The author probably wrote this article to—

Ⓐ tell readers that the Wright brothers flew the first plane.

Ⓑ tell readers about Amelia Earhart's life.

Ⓒ encourage readers to become pilots.

Ⓓ explain the dangers of flying airplanes.

4 Which of the following statements is an opinion?

Ⓕ Amelia admired women with unusual jobs.

Ⓖ Amelia set many records during her lifetime.

Ⓗ Amelia is the greatest woman in history.

Ⓙ Amelia knew she wanted to be a pilot the first time she rode in an airplane.

5 One word that describes Amelia is—

Ⓐ adventurous.

Ⓑ hopeless.

Ⓒ jealous.

Ⓓ timid.

6 Read this sentence from paragraph 7.

She won many awards for her accomplishments and even wrote a book about one of her flights.

Which word means the same as the word **accomplishments**?

Ⓕ journeys

Ⓖ defeats

Ⓗ achievements

Ⓙ goals

GO ON

Practice Reading Test 14—Amelia Earhart

7 Which of the following statements is NOT a fact given in the article?

  Ⓐ Amelia was born in Atchison, Kansas.

  Ⓑ Amelia was the first woman to become a licensed pilot.

  Ⓒ Amelia flew a solo flight across the Atlantic Ocean.

  Ⓓ Amelia didn't like her job at the telephone company.

8 Amelia wanted to fly around the world because she wanted to—

  Ⓕ see other countries.

  Ⓖ break another record.

  Ⓗ prove to her flying instructor that she could do it.

  Ⓙ look for a new place to live.

9 Readers can conclude that during Amelia's last flight,—

  Ⓐ she found a new place to live.

  Ⓑ she decided she didn't want to fly anymore.

  Ⓒ her plane crashed.

  Ⓓ she stayed in New Guinea.

10 Paragraph 5 is mostly about—

  Ⓕ Amelia's childhood.

  Ⓖ how Amelia began to fly.

  Ⓗ Amelia's job at the phone company.

  Ⓙ Amelia's first airplane.

11 This article is—

  Ⓐ an autobiography.

  Ⓑ science fiction.

  Ⓒ a biography.

  Ⓓ historical fiction.

12 Choose the word that correctly completes this sentence.

Amelia and her sister loved to play ball with _____ father.

  Ⓕ their

  Ⓖ there

  Ⓗ they're

  Ⓙ three

STOP

Answer Sheet

STUDENT'S NAME			SCHOOL

LAST | FIRST | MI | TEACHER

GRADE ③ ④ ⑤ ⑥ ⑦ ⑧

FEMALE ○   MALE ○

BIRTH DATE

MONTH	DAY	YEAR

Name bubbles: ○ A B C D E F G H I J K L M N O P Q R S T U V W X Y Z (repeated across all columns)

MONTH	DAY		YEAR	
JAN ○	⓪	⓪	⓪	⓪
FEB ○	①	①	①	①
MAR ○	②	②	②	②
APR ○	③	③	③	③
MAY ○		④	④	④
JUN ○		⑤	⑤	⑤
JUL ○		⑥	⑥	⑥
AUG ○		⑦	⑦	⑦
SEP ○		⑧	⑧	⑧
OCT ○		⑨	⑨	⑨
NOV ○				
DEC ○				

Directions: Mark your answers on this answer sheet. Be sure to fill in each bubble completely and erase any stray marks.

1	Ⓐ Ⓑ Ⓒ Ⓓ	6	Ⓕ Ⓖ Ⓗ Ⓙ	11	Ⓐ Ⓑ Ⓒ Ⓓ
2	Ⓕ Ⓖ Ⓗ Ⓙ	7	Ⓐ Ⓑ Ⓒ Ⓓ	12	Ⓕ Ⓖ Ⓗ Ⓙ
3	Ⓐ Ⓑ Ⓒ Ⓓ	8	Ⓕ Ⓖ Ⓗ Ⓙ	13	Ⓐ Ⓑ Ⓒ Ⓓ
4	Ⓕ Ⓖ Ⓗ Ⓙ	9	Ⓐ Ⓑ Ⓒ Ⓓ	14	Ⓕ Ⓖ Ⓗ Ⓙ
5	Ⓐ Ⓑ Ⓒ Ⓓ	10	Ⓕ Ⓖ Ⓗ Ⓙ	15	Ⓐ Ⓑ Ⓒ Ⓓ

Answer Key

Vocabulary 1
page 6

1 B	7 C
2 J	8 G
3 A	9 B
4 H	10 H
5 B	11 D
6 G	12 J

Vocabulary 2
page 7

1 B	7 C
2 G	8 H
3 A	9 C
4 H	10 F
5 D	11 D
6 H	12 J

Vocabulary 3
page 8

1 B	7 B
2 H	8 J
3 B	9 A
4 G	10 H
5 C	11 B
6 H	12 J

4 Mike and Moe
page 9

1 A	7 C
2 J	8 G
3 C	9 C
4 G	10 F
5 B	11 C
6 J	12 G

13 The student should create a correct Venn diagram. One possible example to include: Mike is independent, Moe is timid, they are both cats.

5 Neighbors Need Neighbors
page 12

1 C	7 A
2 F	8 H
3 B	9 D
4 F	10 J
5 B	11 C
6 G	12 G

6 Sharks
page 15

1 A	7 C
2 G	8 H
3 C	9 B
4 H	10 G
5 C	11 A
6 F	12 H

13 The student should use correct outline format to show the main points about sharks including, for example, myths about sharks, types of sharks, the biology of sharks, and how sharks hunt.

7 Emilio's Tadpoles
page 18

1 C	9 A
2 F	10 F
3 D	11 B
4 H	12 G
5 D	13 C
6 H	14 J
7 B	15 D
8 F	

16 Accept any reasonable response that incorporates information about Emilio, his family, the setting, and his situation. Endings should fit the genre of the story.

8 The Midnight Ride
page 22

1 A	7 A
2 F	8 H
3 C	9 B
4 J	10 H
5 B	11 C
6 G	12 G

9 Saguaro Cactus
page 25

1 B	7 C
2 J	8 F
3 C	9 C
4 G	10 G
5 B	11 C
6 G	12 H

13 Accept any reasonable version of the saguaro's life cycle that is based on facts from the article. Make sure the student has placed the facts in chronological order.

10 A Field Trip to the Recycling Center
page 28

1 D	9 C
2 G	10 G
3 C	11 A
4 H	12 H
5 C	13 D
6 H	14 G
7 B	15 B
8 G	

11 Stained Light
page 32

1 A	9 D
2 G	10 H
3 D	11 D
4 H	12 J
5 C	13 B
6 H	14 F
7 C	15 C
8 F	

12 A Class Trip to the Zoo
page 36

1 B	9 B
2 F	10 G
3 C	11 D
4 J	12 G
5 A	13 B
6 H	14 H
7 B	15 A
8 H	

13 Another Use for Seeds
page 40

1 B	7 A
2 F	8 J
3 C	9 C
4 F	10 H
5 A	11 D
6 H	12 H

14 Amelia Earhart
page 43

1 A	7 D
2 H	8 G
3 B	9 C
4 H	10 G
5 A	11 C
6 H	12 F